BOLTON

BOLTON

Susanne Baillie
Alanna May
Isabelle Schmelzer

THE BOSTON MILLS PRESS

Queen Street around 1910. Why are all the cars parked on the wrong side of the road?

Canadian Cataloguing in Publication Data

Baillie, Susanne
  Bolton

Includes index.
ISBN 1-55046-036-6

1. Bolton (Ont.) – History.   I. May, Alanna.
II. Schmelzer, Isabelle.   III. Title.

FC3099.B64B34 1989   971.3'535   C89-094074-6
F1059.5.B64B34 1989

© Boston Mills Press, 1989

Published by:
THE BOSTON MILLS PRESS
132 Main Street
Erin, Ontario N0B 1T0
TEL (519) 833-2407
FAX (519) 833-2195

American Association
for State and Local History
Award of Merit

Winners of the
Heritage Canada
Communications Award

Design by John Denison
Cover Design by Gill Stead
Typeset by Speed River Graphics
Printed by Ampersand, Guelph

The publisher wishes to acknowledge the financial assistance and encouragement of The Canada Council, the Ontario Arts Council and the Office of the Secretary of State.

O.M. Hodson hardware store, 1896-1906.

CONTENTS

7	Foreword
9	Introduction
11	Business in Bolton
35	Homes
42	Street Scenes
49	Railway
50	Churches
56	Public Buildings
61	Bolton's Reeves
65	Schools
71	Floods
75	Robertson Matthews
77	Special Events and Sports
86	Did You Know…
91	Acknowledgements
92	Index

Bolton Orange Day Parade, July 12, 1911.

FOREWORD

The study of local history has been part of school social studies for only a comparatively short period of time. Now that we are in the late 1980s, it is generally appreciated that to know what a community is going to look like and what it will be like in the 21st century, one must also understand what it was like in the past. The evolution that has occurred and will continue to occur also gives students a sense of identity.

Local history study involves an appreciation of prehistory, the contact periods between natives and early arrivals from Europe, the impact of settlement on the landscape, and the dramatic change from an agricultural-based community to an industrial one where transportation and communication became the pivotal points of everyone's existence. These studies can include geography, natural history, and use the visual arts.

Humberview Secondary School is typical of the many newer schools in Peel. Its construction was the direct result of the dramatic population growth in our region. Like many other schools, few of the students and their families, or their teachers, actually originated in this community historically referred to as Albion and Bolton, now Wards Four and Five of the town of Caledon. The study that led to this publication, therefore, became a wonderful opportunity for the new school to become part of the whole community. When it started, no one could have fully appreciated how well it would bridge the gap and forge links between the old and new. Archival studies, oral histories, research, cemetery and genealogical studies, liasons with the local historical society and municipal heritage advisory committee, and visits to the regional museum and archives also furnished exceptional educational opportunities. Indeed, some of the young people who initiated this project have gone out into the world beyond the classroom armed, we trust, with the confidence, gained from a knowledge and appreciation of their roots, to meet new people without shyness and to be able to offer their employer skills and abilities that they developed while working on the project and on this book.

Warmest congratulations must be extended to all of the students, their families, the principals and teaching staff, and the residents of the community who contributed through oral histories and the loan of precious material and old photographs. Every one of you has created something unique and special for your very own secondary school and your community.

Heather R. Broadbent
Chairman, Caledon Heritage Committee
Director, Ontario Heritage Committee
November 1988

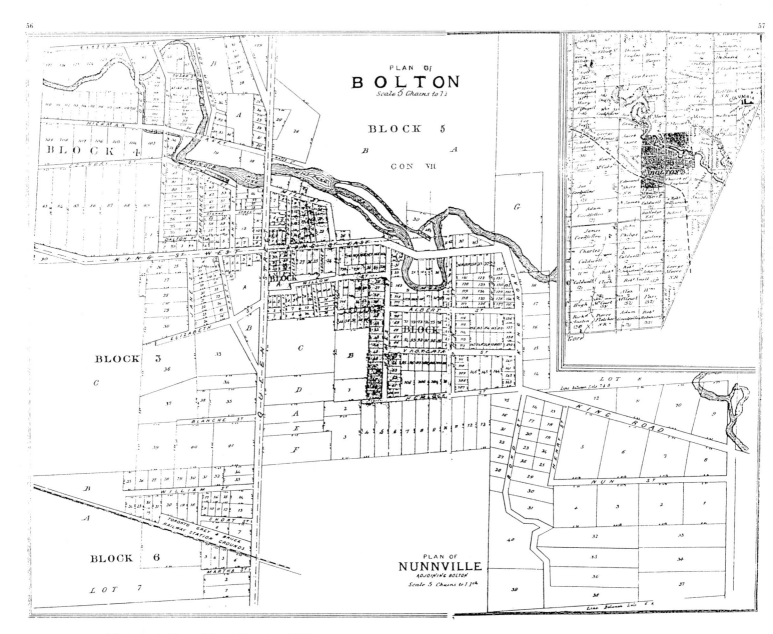

Historical Atlas of Peel County, 1877.

INTRODUCTION
A BRIEF HISTORY OF BOLTON

Almost two centuries ago, the area in which Bolton is now situated was hilly, rugged, yet beautiful terrain intersected by the freely flowing Humber River. Its sole inhabitants were Indians (who frequently passed through the area in canoes or, in winter, on snowshoes and handsleighs) and the numerous forms of wildlife, including an abundance of deer, fish and bears.

The arrival of James Bolton from Norfolk, England, in 1818 was to gradually transform this area into the bustling village of Bolton. Following the arrival of his nephew, George Bolton, in 1820, a mill site was selected, and shortly thereafter a small, frame grist mill was constructed. Soon known as "Bolton's Mill," the area began to attract settlers, and by 1840 it boasted 14 houses, 2 stores, blacksmiths, shoemakers, a tailor, and a hotel.

Nonetheless, those lured by the promise of a better life in Canada found that life as an immigrant was not easy. It was hard work clearing acres of land covered in dense brush, forests and raspberry bushes. In addition, the summers were short, frost came early, and unexpected snowstorms seemed to appear from nowhere. However, these experiences built character and brought the community together in a strong sense of unity. Logging bees, "quiltings" and barn-raisings were held in high spirits, and often ended in hearty celebrations.

"Bolton's Mill" continued to prosper and shape a unique identity of its own, enduring floods and fires, yet continuing to expand. In 1872 it was decided that the village of Bolton should become a separate entity and no longer belong to the township of Albion. In accordance with this change, a Town Council was elected in January 1873, with Lambert L. Bolton at its head, and also having the honour of being the first reeve of the village of Bolton.

In the years that followed, Bolton saw the founding, and often the downfall, of such prominent businesses and organizations as Walshaw Woollen Mills, the Toronto, Grey & Bruce railway station, the Bolton Foundry, the Albert Street school, the *Enterprise*, various hotels, the Imperial Bank of Canada, Bolton Big Band, and many more.

Those who reside in Bolton today are living in a strong community started by those first determined settlers. Just as those first settlers once did, today we are watching the community grow, change and further develop. These changes continue to cultivate Bolton's own unique identity begun in the rolling Albion hills and the scenic Humber River valley.

As you turn the pages of this book, imagine yourself riding in a time capsule, and experience first-hand the stories which lie behind each person and building that have shaped Bolton.

Isabelle Schmelzer

A.E. McCabe, general blacksmith, circa 1910.

BUSINESS IN BOLTON

In the late 1800s, Bolton had a large number of successful businesses.

The most important was McFall's flour mill, run by Andrew and Arthur McFall. It was capable of grinding 150 to 200 barrels of flour daily. McFall's shipped out barrels of flour to other towns as well as supplying the home market.

There was a second type of mill in Bolton, Walshaw's Woollen Mills. They manufactured such items as woollen clothes and blankets.

In 1869 Mr. Dick started his agricultural works on Ann Street. It started off as a fairly small business, but soon enlarged. There was hardly an agricultural implement that Mr. Dick didn't manufacture.

Mr. A. Dodds began his carriage works in 1873. He manufactured very well-made items.

Also around this time there were four dry goods stores in Bolton. They were owned by E.A. Jaffary, Thomas Fisher, James Clarke and A.E. Harper. Mr. Fisher sold hardware along with his groceries.

Mr. G. Nunn dealt in all types of sewing machines, organs and pianos. He had many agents across the country who sold these items for him.

There were three tailor shops in Bolton in the late 1800s. They were owned by C.A. Martin, R. Kenyon and Joe Wilson. There were also two harness shops.

At one time there were five hotels here. Thomas Curliss owned the Albion Hotel over the bridge to the north. Hassards kept a mud-brick hotel a little back of where the *Enterprise* is today. It burned in a spectacular fire on Fall Fair night in 1872. There were many proprietors of the Ontario House Hotel, including Richard Beamish. It was located where Main Street station is now. Ontario House burned down in 1916. George Evans owned the Exchange Hotel, later Queen's Hotel. It was located where the Bonanza parking lot is today and burned down in 1969. Finally, there was the Masonic Arms Hotel located on the present site of the Canadian Imperial Bank of Commerce. It was owned by William Curliss and had two other names, Star and Balmoral.

R.J. Russell had the only jewellery store in Bolton. He kept a wonderful stock of watches, clocks, etc.

J.P. Plummer had the foundry on Mill Street where the Hydro office is now located.

There were three blacksmith shops and five shoemaking shops in Bolton.

F.N. Leavens ran the printing office. He turned out first-class printing as well as the local paper, the *Enterprise*.

This photo shows the McFall cottage (white house at right), McFall dam, the mill office, and the mill itself.

McFall's Dam, Bolton.

THE BOLTON MILL

In 1818 James Bolton came to settle here, and in 1823 he relieved many nearby settlers by setting up a dam and a small frame grist mill on Lot 9 Concession 7, Albion (now the round corner of Mill Street).

In 1842 his nephew, George Bolton, bought this mill property from him, and two years later moved the mill to its hill site (what is now the corner of Humberlea Road and King Street East).

In 1850 an addition was built onto the mill. At the same time, a building known as McFall's cottage (which still stands on King Street East) and some stables were erected.

Four years later, in 1854, the mill property was sold to Edward Lawson, who in turn sold it to John Gardhouse in 1859. Mr. Gardhouse expanded his mill business until, by 1870, the mill had a daily output of 125 barrels of flour.

In 1881 the mill was sold to Andrew McFall. Mr. McFall died in 1894, so his son Arthur took over. The McFall family had ownership of the mill for about 46 years, until in 1940 the Hayhoe brothers of Woodbridge bought it. In 1959 the Hayhoe brothers sold it to some Woodbridge farmers, who later sold it again.

On April 21, 1968, it was decided that the mill was to be dismantled. In order to provide practice for the local firemen, the mill was set on fire first. When the fire was extinguished, they continued with the dismantling.

The first picture shows the mill as it was when the McFall family ran it. The second picture shows the same view of the mill during the dismantling of it on April 21, 1968.

The mill in Bolton was quite a landmark. In the winter, children dragged their toboggans over the hill by the mill to go sledding. When Reverend Featherstone Lake Osler visited town, he would stop by to preach in the empty wheat bin. The Bolton Mill put Bolton on the map and was the start of a growing community.

These Norton Brickworks employees took time out for this photo. They are, left to right: Jack White, William Stewart, Fred Stubbs, Alsoy Norton, William "Skinny Bill" Robertson, and George Norton.

NORTON'S BRICKWORKS

The brickworks were started in 1845 by Matthew Grey. The plant was located by the south end of what is now David Street. David Street was originally used as the lane down which the bricks were carted in wagons. This accounts for the narrowness of the road.

In 1850 the brickworks were sold to David Norton, the person David Street was named after. Mr. Norton's son Alsey conducted the business. The Norton family was experienced in brickmaking, as the family had been brickmakers for several generations in England and Canada.

It was hard work being a brickmaker. The hours were long and the tasks exhausting. Bricks were made using a special machine. Two horses were used to draw the large beams around, while one man fed the machine with wet, processed clay which was free of rubble. The clay came out into a brickmold holding five bricks each, and these bricks were dusted with a mixture of red mortar and sand. The bricks were turned out on a pallet board and wheeled into hocks to dry. If there was clear, dry weather, the bricks would generally be dry enough to be put into the kiln for about one week of steady firing. About 1880, one thousand of these bricks went for $6. A fine example of bricks from Norton's Brickworks can be found at St. James Cathedral in Toronto.

The David Norton residence can still be seen at 116 Meadowvale Court in downtown Bolton.

THE QUEEN'S HOTEL

In 1835 George Evans located in Bolton. At first he owned a small log house and shoemaking shop on the corner of Sterne and Queen streets. In 1845 he built the Exchange Hotel on the present site of the Bonanza supermarket on Queen Street. After the hotel was destroyed by fire in 1881, he rebuilt it, larger and better, with verandas on the front and sides. It was the best hotel of the five or six in Bolton, with the best dining room and bedrooms. The hotel was used by all commercial men and a large share of the farmers. Also, the shed and stables behind the hotel, directed by James Morrison, were publicly used.

Soon after Evans reopened the hotel, he sold it to T.D. Elliott, who had married Evans' youngest daughter, Helen. Elliott changed the name to Queen's Hotel before he sold it in 1920 to Floyd Henderson. In 1930 Henderson sold the hotel to Frank and Norman Clarke. Then, in 1945, they sold the hotel to Mike Broetski and William Greshuk, who converted it to apartments and a restaurant. Eventually Broetski became sole owner, and he sold the hotel to the Kuniski brothers in the 1960s. The Kuniski brothers were the owners when the hotel burned in 1969. The fire was blamed on careless smoking. All 15 residents of the hotel were evacuated safely. Only one resident, Dave Harper, suffered injury, receiving slight burns to his hands. The remnants were eventually torn down.

Shown here is the Queen's Hotel. It was built by George Evans in 1881. At bottom right, beer barrels can be seen being brought into the hotel.

The Ontario House Hotel in 1911.

THE ONTARIO HOUSE HOTEL

This hotel was built in 1856 on the east side of Queen Street where Main Street Station is now located. The hotel was first kept by a lame man, Mr. McKee, and it was noted for its extremely good meals. Mr. McKee eventually sold out to W.J. Dixon. The hotel was later owned by Richard Beamish, J. Squires, T. Linfoot, and W. Tedor. Daniel Small father of Ambrose Small, a Toronto millionaire who mysteriously disappeared, was also proprietor for a while.

In 1916 the hotel burned down. Because the fire covered everything in a thick, black soot, parents were advised not to allow their children to attend school. The lot remained empty until after WWII, when Egan Hardware and Furniture was established there. Egan's was later moved to the corner of Queen and Mill streets.

This is Queen Street looking north. Jaffary's store is the first one on the left side.

JAFFARY'S GENERAL STORE

In 1857 Wyatt Jaffary moved to Bolton from Macville. Soon after his arrival he purchased the Prossor place, which was located on the corner of King and Mill streets. He also bought a partnership with J. McIlroy. McIlroy had a small store on the northwest corner of King and Queen streets. A few years later Jaffary bought out McIlroy's interest. He then moved the old store back and built a large frame store in its place. He sold it in 1893 and moved it off to make room for the present brick store.

Jaffary continued selling groceries and dry goods for several years, then his sons Edwin and Wyatt, Jr. assumed the responsibilities under the name E.A. Jaffary. The telegraph office was located here and run by the Jaffarys until the arrival of the railroad. The telegraph received daily weather reports from the central office of the Meteorological Service in Toronto.

The partnership of Edwin and Wyatt, Jr. continued for 50 years, until Edwin became sick and retired. Wyatt, Jr. and Dan Fines then formed a partnership. When Wyatt, Jr. retired, his place was taken by Alex Barry. Barry and Fines continued their partnership until Fines died in January 1946. Earl Small assumed Fines' position in October 1947. Alex Barry's half of the business was eventually bought by Teddy Houston. Small and Houston dissolved their partnership in January 1951, at which time Houston became the sole owner. This store is now the variety store Your Convenience.

LEGGETT & SMITH DRUGSTORE

This drugstore is located on the northeast corner of King and Queen streets. It was built in 1854 by James C. Stork as a drug and seed store. Samuel J. Snell bought the building in 1886. He operated it as a drugstore and post office after his was destroyed in a large fire the same year. When a new store was built on the former site, he moved into it. There was a store called the Emporium, owned by Mr. Hughes, in this building at one time.

Mr. C.A. Leggett came to Bolton in 1932 or 1933, bought the building and opened a drugstore. It had been empty for a while before he arrived.

This is C.A. Leggett's drugstore on the northeast corner of King and Queen streets. The photo was taken by the proprietor, C.A. Leggett.

Here is a photo of 49 Queen Street North when it was Cameron's store. Honey's Men's Shop is presently located here. The upper rooms were used as the meeting place for Miss Maggie O'Dea's three-month course.

CAMERON'S VARIETY

This store was built in 1860 by Mr. John Gardhouse and opened for business that same year. When Mr. Gardhouse died in 1878, his wife and son Fred kept the business going for three more years.

In 1881 James Clarke purchased the building and ran a general store called Mammoth, using an elephant as a trademark. Upstairs, on the second floor, Miss Maggie O'Dea owned and operated a dressmaker's shop.

There were many owners after James Clarke, including Mr. Purvis, Mr. Staples and Mr. Ellwood. When Mr. Ellwood retired, the store was taken over by the partnership of Love & Cameron. After two years the partnership was dissolved, and Bruce Cameron was left to keep the store going. In 1953 a grocery line carried on there as Cameron's Variety. Honey's Men's Shop is presently located there.

During the winter of 1921-22, Miss Maggie O'Dea ran a three-month short course on the second floor of this building. In the first month, Mrs. Bertha Duncan taught food values and practical cooking. In the second month, home nursing, first aid, child study and mothercraft were taught by Mrs. Lowe. And in the third month, Miss Edith Collins instructed sewing, adjusting patterns, cutting and fitting. Other subjects taught during this course included such things as English, arithmetic, animal husbandry and poultry. At the end of the course there was an examination to test what the ladies had learned.

Ladies enrolled in Miss Maggie O'Dea's course in 1921.

Workers from the Dick Foundry. Top left, Harry Sheardown. Bottom, second from left, Jimmy Stubbs.

BOLTON IRON WORKS

In 1869 J.P. Plummer became the newest resident of Bolton. He took control of the moulding and casting department of the William Dick Agricultural Works, where he remained until 1878, when it was destroyed by fire. In that same year, Mr. Plummer rebuilt his foundry, relocating on the lot next to the pond on Queen Street, with George Watson as a partner. Unfortunately, the new business was not a success, and Mr. Watson retired. Mr. Plummer then moved his residence to a lot on Mill Street.

Soon after, his son William Plummer built the Mill Street foundry and equipped it with the machinery necessary to operate. He then turned the company over to his father. With the help of his other son, Charles, J.P. ran it for one year, at which time William decided to join his father and brother in the business. J.P. Plummer died in 1893, but Charles and William kept up the family business as a partnership until just before WWII. At this time the foundry went broke, and Howard Furnace took over for a short while. Eventually, the Town Council bought the property to use as the Hydro building.

At first the work done by the foundry was mainly plows and beams, but later was expanded to furnaces and general cast-iron work, as well as the repairing of farm machinery.

From the Historical Atlas of Peel County, 1877.

BOLTON CARRIAGE WORKS

Born in 1847, Mr. Albert Dodds learned the carriage-making trade in the village of Kettleby. He came to Bolton in 1873, and in that same year built the Bolton Carriage Works, located on the southeast corner of King and Eliza streets. This is where Bolton Builders once stood, now the site of the new downtown mall.

Bolton Carriage Works was known throughout the counties of Peel and York for producing buggies of high quality, with excellent style, durability and finish. On several occasions these buggies won prizes at township and county fair exhibitions.

In 1913 Mr. Egan bought the carriage works and undertaking from Mr. Dodds. The undertaking business was run in the same building as the carriage works, as someone could not make a decent living off the undertaking alone.

BOLTON CARRIAGE WORKS, A. DODDS PROPR BOLTON, ALBION, P.O.

Bolton Carriage Works.

Mr. Albert Dodds (driver's seat) and passengers outside the Bolton Carriage Works.

Here is one of the five Walshaw Woollen Mills, all of which were destroyed by fire. In this photo, blankets can be seen drying out front.

WALSHAW'S WOOLLEN MILLS

The mill was located on the present-day Glasgow Road near the river. Situated on a level piece of land in the valley on the west side of the Humber River in the northwest section of Bolton, the building looked up at the highlands surrounding it. It was in the centre of Glasgow, which was a suburb of Bolton, then called Bolton Hollow or Bolton Mills. It is presumed that the first owner of the mill, John F. McIntosh, had something to do with the name Glasgow, since he was from Scotland.

John McIntosh purchased the land on Glasgow Road in 1855. He bought water power on the river and constructed a residence and a woollen mill. Early documents indicate good business in wool carding, and the mill employed ten men.

In October 1863 Alexander and William Buist bought the property. During their ownership, Glasgow was taken in as part of Bolton. (This was accomplished on June 3, 1872, when the population was slightly less than 900.) The Buists also constructed a sawmill.

Joshua Walshaw was an Englishman who located in Bolton in 1882. He purchased the mill buildings on July 19, 1882. He was regarded as a keen businessman, and he also served as a councillor in 1884 and 1889. His son Edward assisted him in the business.

On Tuesday, August 11, 1896, at 10 o'clock, Joshua Walshaw visited the mill to discover a fire in the second storey of the frame building. He sounded the alarm, but it was impossible to save the building. The sawmill, bleach houses and lumber belonging to farmers, as well as 50 cords of wood, were also destroyed. The total loss amounted to $25,000. Only Robert Fox's home and the storehouse full of newly made blankets were saved. Soon after the fire, a thunderstorm hit, blowing burning shingles as far as Tingley Monument Works on King Street East.

Mr. Walshaw was confined to his bed because of the tragedy, but after his recovery he announced his plan to rebuild. In the latter part of 1896 he constructed a three-storey brick building.

On Tuesday, March 24, 1903, the mill caught fire again. After the fire was put out, only tottery brick walls and twisted machinery remained. Late that summer the Walshaws rebuilt.

When Joshua Walshaw retired, his son Edward took over the business. In the summer of 1904 Edward constructed another building at Glasgow. It was also destroyed by fire. Soon after this fire, Edward rebuilt for the final time. This mill was destroyed by fire on Wednesday, July 4, 1923.

The Imperial Bank of Canada building was built in 1906 on the southeast corner of King and Queen streets.

IMPERIAL BANK OF CANADA

Generally, no cash was used in Old Bolton except in the hotels. Everything was done by credit or by trade.

Mr. Fawcett and Mr. VanDeusen opened a private bank on the corner of Queen and Sterne streets in Pearcy Block. It was sold to John F. Warbrick, whose sister Daisy was a teller.

In 1903 John F. Warbrick, who had contacts with the Imperial Bank, looked into a matter concerning the Sovereign Bank of Toronto's interest in opening a bank in Bolton. As a result, the Imperial Bank was established in Bolton with Warbrick as manager.

In 1906 the Imperial Bank secured an option on hotel property on the southeast corner of King and Queen streets. This hotel was called the Masonic Arms, also known as the Balmoral and the Star.

In 1906 the bank building pictured was built. The Imperial Bank had five managers up to 1972. They were John F. Warbrick, Charles C. Case, Mr. Robinson, Alex Hutchinson and Reg Pacey.

On June 1, 1961, the Imperial Bank of Canada and the Canadian Bank of Commerce consolidated and are now known as the Canadian Imperial Bank of Commerce or the CIBC.

SMITH & SCHAEFER HARDWARE

The Smith & Schaefer hardware store was a local business situated at 56 Queen Street North. The store sold stoves and ranges, paints, shovels, lamps, and furnaces, to name a few items. The senior member of the partnership was an Englishman by the name of Mr. Robert Smith, and the junior member was Mr. Alex Schaefer.

Previous to Smith & Schaefer, there was another hardware store, O.M. Hodson's, located in the same building. The building itself shares a common wall with the Bolton Enterprise, just to the left of what was Smith & Schaefer and what is now Cowieson's. Home Hardware was located there previous to Cowieson's.

Smith and Schaefer hardware store circa 1910, 56 Queen Street North.

This is Frank N. Leavens, who was hired by H.H. Bolton to run the Enterprise. Mr. Leavens bought the Enterprise in 1893.

This is Werden Leavens, who inherited the Enterprise from his father, F.N. Leavens. He was publisher and editor of the paper from 1940 to 1976.

BOLTON NEWSPAPERS

The first newspaper to serve Bolton was called the *Cardwell Observer*. It was published in 1871 by J.N. Bolton. For a while the *Cardwell Observer* was the subject of a great deal of negative criticism and comments. There were many hoaxes set up to try and catch its editor.

In the beginning the entire office staff consisted of one man, who served as editor, printer and compositor of the newspaper. The only other person on staff was the young boy hired to run the ink rollers for a few hours on publishing day. Everything needed to run the newspaper was located in one building. There were two presses in the office, one small Gordon pedal press for printing cards, billheads and small dodgers, and an old hand press for printing the newspaper and large posters.

Later on, around 1886, the name of the paper was changed to the *British Standard*. During 1888 the paper, whose office was located where the Riverside Restaurant and Tavern are now located, was discontinued. The business was sold to H.H. Bolton, who moved it to a location on Queen Street North and changed the name to the Bolton *Enterprise*. Since H.H. Bolton had little experience as a newspaper publisher, he hired F.N. Leavens, a capable 18-year-old from Pickering, to manage the paper. Mr. Bolton was very glad to have Frank Leavens, since at that time he was reeve of Bolton as well as being publisher of the paper, and was quite busy. F.N. Leavens was

British Standard,
AND CARDWELL ADVERTISER.

"In things essential, Unity; in things doubtful, Liberty; in all things, Charity."

BOLTON, ONT., FRIDAY, JUNE 19th, 1874.

County Council.

From the 'Peel Banner.'

The County Council met on Monday afternoon last, when the following members were present: Mr. Gooderham, Chairman of the Select Committee appointed to repair the Caslor Bridge over the Credit between Toronto Township and Streetsville, presented a eventually received three memorials... Mr. Chisholm stated that some arrangement would be necessary to meet the incurring expenses, confirming two by-laws passed by Caledon Council enabling them to dispose of certain road allowances not required, confirmation by the County Council being required by

---

hired in 1889, and in 1893 he decided to purchase the *Enterprise* from H.H. Bolton, for $750. The building in which the *Enterprise* plant was located was being rented for $50 a year.

In November 1900 F.N. Leavens and his wife bought 50 Queen Street North from Alfred Harper for $1,600. Mr. Harper had previously used the building for his general store. The *Enterprise* moved in during 1901, and the Leavens lived upstairs.

F.N. Leavens died in 1941, and in his will he left his son Werden the newspaper. Werden Leavens successfully ran the paper until 1976, when it was sold to a company called Metrospan. By April 1984 the company was called Metroland, and the *Enterprise* was sold to Bill McCutcheon, who is the present publisher. The actual printing plant has not left Leavens' hands since 1893, three generations. After 98 years, it can safely be said that the Leavens' printing plant is the oldest continuous family-run business in Bolton.

Early editions of the Bolton *Enterprise* consisted of about four pages of solid writing, with ads but no photos. Two pages were set aside for international news, and the remaining two were left for the typical gossip found locally. Featured in the paper were items known as "localettes," which were just small pieces of gossip and local incidents. Here are a few samples of "localettes":

- The lawns and flower gardens in Bolton never looked better than they do at present.
- Kenneth, aged 11, son of Mr. Normad Rowley, had his foot badly injured when a horse stepped on it while the lad was watering the horses.
- Mrs. Robert Elliott, of Toronto, is spending a few days with Bolton friends.

The Dick brothers, Alex and Albert, had the first threshing machine in Bolton, in 1906. It was a J.I. Case steam engine and separator. This scene was at Bob Williamson's threshing in 1909. The Dicks lived on Huntington Road, one and a half miles north of Nashville.

THE BOLTON MARKET

An event of great importance, especially to farmers, was the thriving Monday morning market. Beginning circa 1905, cries of "Get your fresh eggs here!" could be heard each Monday morning in front of the Town Hall beginning at 10 a.m. and ending at noon. Products such as butter and eggs were considered staple produce and were available year round. Items such as fruit, honey, dressed mutton and beef could be found at different times of year. Animals such as geese, chickens and turkeys were sold seasonally according to festive occasions. Although consumers sometimes paid higher prices for staple products, buyers were known to come from as far as Toronto on a regular basis, and also from Nobleton, Palgrave and Sandhill. Due to it being a wholesale market (you couldn't buy just one pound of butter, you had to buy at least five) and the fact that it was very busy, one couldn't pay upon receipt of goods. Instead, the buyer gave the farmer a slip of paper stating how much he had bought in pounds and of what item. The bank then figured the cost and paid the money from the buyer's account. When the Bolton market ceased to exist, circa 1927, it was greatly missed by both the citizens of Bolton and those of nearby communities.

JENNIE BELL HOME

This building has been demolished, but was located approximately where the Royal Bank is now. It was used for many years by Mr. J. Bell, a conveyancer. He was assisted by his daughter, Jennie Bell, who operated the telegraph lines that ran from the railway station to their home.

Later, this building was used by a Mr. R.I. Russell as a store. His store sold many glass dishes, gifts and postcards with pictures of Bolton on them. The Russells lived in the building located on the southeast corner of James and Albert streets, which was originally built for Lambert Bolton, Bolton's first reeve.

Dr. W.J. McCabe, a veterinarian, also had his office and home here at one time, and made many improvements to the structure. He lived here for many years, until it was bought by H.O. (Ted) Houston. Mr. Houston had great plans, but they were never carried out because of illness and subsequent death. H.O. Houston was the man for whom the downtown Ted Houston Park was named.

At one time this building was tagged the "Purple Peril" (for reasons withheld by the authors).

T.A. Dick Garage, Queen Street North.

This picture shows the Dick home in its original state. The people in the picture are, from left to right, William Dick, Edith Burton, Thomson Alexander Dick, Florence Dick and Andrew Dick.

THE DICK HOME

The Dick home is located at 49 Sterne Street. The owner of this building was Thomson Alexander Dick, the son of William Dick. In 1869 William Dick built a large machine shop and foundry called William Dick Agricultural Works, which unfortunately burned down in 1878. He built another machine shop and foundry, which burned down also.

The John Verner house, which was situated on King Street East until its demolition to make way for the new downtown mall.

This is the Charles Plummer residence, which still stands at the corner of James and Albert streets. The "White Lily" pattern fence out front was one of the products made at the foundry. One day a couple of boys dragged hockey sticks along the top of the fence and knocked the tiny lilies off. Only one remains today. Try finding it if you happen to drive by.

Goodfellow House, King Street East.

This home, which still stands on the southeast corner of James and Albert streets, is over 100 years old. It was built for Bolton's first reeve, Lambert Bolton. Bolton served as reeve for the years 1875 to 1877, and again in 1880 and 1881.

Bolton circa 1910.

Back, left to right: George, Rebecca, Ernie, Dill, May and Jim Stewart. Front, left to right: Andrew and Elizy Stewart.

Bolton, looking north.

Humber River bridge on Queen Street North, 1908, near present-day Mr. Submarine.

Queen Street, looking north.

Queen Street, looking north, somewhat later. What differences do you see?

When minor road repairs were necessary, they would often be done using a simple machine such as the one shown. This scraper would be used for things such as grading the dirt roads. This photo was taken looking at C.A. Leggett's drugstore on the northeast corner of Queen and King streets.

This photo was taken looking south on Queen Street and shows the construction the well-used road underwent in 1930. This enormous hill was straightened until a road had been cut through the top. The route created was offered as an alternate to the previous one, which ran south along Queen Street as far as Elizabeth, west along Elizabeth, and south along Nancy to the top of the hill. With the arrival of automobiles, it was no longer necessary to provide a curved road to help horses up the steep hill.

Dr. and Mrs. Hickman lived on Queen Street, so they saw many of the teamsters heading to the city. Mrs. Hickman's parrot learned to swear beautifully by listening to the teamsters. One day, when Rev. H.B. Osler called on Mrs. Hickman, he was greeted by the parrot's newly learned profanities. Mrs. Hickman could only stop the bird by throwing an apron over its cage. When the south end of Queen Street was straightened, automobiles replaced the daily parade of teamsters, and both the Hickmans and their parrot heard substantially less cursing.

This is the Bolton railway station built by the Toronto, Grey and Bruce Railway. To the right can be seen the Queen's Hotel carriage.

THE TORONTO, GREY & BRUCE RAILWAY

It was in December 1870 that the first train ran from Toronto to Bolton, at a whopping 25 m.p.h. The route, not completed until 1873, was different than the route known today, for the C.P.R. changed it in 1908. The first station, located on the north side of Ellwood Drive, just east of the Baptist church, was looked after by Bryan Dowling, who had the honour of being the first stationmaster. Making his home in the living quarters of the station, he was busy almost 24 hours a day handling large loads of freight, express and telegraph messages.

Besides offering transportation of goods, the T.G. & B. ran a train to Toronto every day from this station. To accommodate the many people who made use of this "link" to Toronto, the Queen's Hotel ran a carriage service from the hotel to the station starting circa 1873.

Although the station made the movement of goods such as grain and flour much easier and more economical, it also brought on a negative economic situation in Bolton. Due to the fact that the trains made it so easy to travel to Toronto, much business and commerce that could have been accomplished in Bolton was done in Toronto. Therefore, not as much money was spent in Bolton in the late 1880s, local businesses experienced a decline in sales, and the town's rate of economic growth fell for a short period of time.

On August 1, 1883, it was announced that the T.G. & B. had been leased to the Ontario & Quebec Railway, which in turn was a branch of the C.P.R. In 1908 the C.P.R. changed the route through Bolton to its present location. The existing station was built at its present location on Ellwood Drive West, with the old station remaining in use as a freight shed for many years. In keeping with the tremendous changes occurring in 1908, a line from Bolton to Sudbury was constructed and opened.

Meanwhile, Bryan Dowling's urge to further aid the community increased and Bolton's first "pioneer" telegraph system was constructed. This system ran from the first railway station to the home which then belonged to Jennie Bell. With her father, a conveyancer, she operated this telegraph line successfully until the onset of more advanced technology.

From the minute the first train chugged into Bolton in 1870, to the hour when it was announced as an important link with the C.P.R., to the day of the closure of the second station, the railway stations served the community well and will always be remembered as important factors in the growth of Bolton.

CHRIST CHURCH

Before churches were built in Bolton, the Reverend Adam Elliott was the travelling missionary in Albion. He conducted services on the threshing floor of Boyce Sterne's barn in 1834. In 1837 the Reverend Featherstone Lake Osler was appointed as the new missionary, but in 1843 he returned to England to continue his studies. At this time his younger brother, the Reverend Henry Bath Osler, was appointed to take his place. Reverend Osler directed the construction of Bolton's first mud-brick church. It was situated on the west side of Highway 50 at Bolton's north end. Its original cemetery can still be seen on Centennial Drive. James and Ellen Bolton and Samuel and Anne Sterne gave the land to the church. The church itself was built in 1845. In 1848 the mud church was replaced by a frame building. In 1872 the present brick church was erected on Nancy Street. This land was given by James Stork.

One interesting feature in the history of the church is its association with neighbouring Anglican churches.

From 1844-75 Christ Church combined with Lloydtown to make the Parish of Bolton. Also around this time they combined with Pine Grove, Sandhill, St. James, Albion and Nobleton. In later years this combination continued: From 1876-92, St. Mark's, Sandhill; 1893-1917, St. Alban's, Palgrave; 1918-55, St. Mary's, Tullamore; 1956 to present, St. John's, Castlemore.

Incumbents
1843-1875	Rev. Canon H.B. Osler
1875-1885	Rev. W.N. Clarke
1885-1890	Rev. E.A. Oliver
1890-1892	Rev. W. Cassisis-Kennedy
1892-1894	Rev. William Walsh
1894-1896	Rev. E.M. Pickford
1896-1900	Rev. H.M. Little
1900-1903	Rev. R.J. Coleman
1903-1908	Rev. Joseph Fletcher
1908-1917	Rev. W.E. Westney
1917-1927	Rev. P.N. Knight
1927-1936	Rev. Frank Herman
1936-1951	Rev. J.J. Robbins
1951-1953	Rev. R.H. Howson
1953-1956	Rev. P.C. Howard
1956-1960	Rev. J.S. Crouch
1960-1970	Rev. Harvey Markle
1971-1975	Rev. Robert Leckey
1975-1982	Rev. J.W.B. Hill
1982-1987	Rev. Douglas A. Stoute
1987-	Rev. Dana Johnston

This is the original interior of Christ Church, showing the altar and three of the windows.

The Reverend Canon Henry Bath Osler of Christ Church, Bolton's first official priest.

When the church was built in 1872, the interior was constructed in traditional Anglican style. The centre aisle led to a raised chancel with an altar bearing a brass cross and candlesticks behind the communion rail in the sanctuary. Stained-glass windows in the church add colour and are memorials to former congregation members. The centre window depicts Christ and was given by the vestry in the 1880s. The left window depicts St. John the Evangelist and was given in memory of Isabella Johnston. The right window depicts St. Peter and was given in memory of Robert William Johnston. A window on the west side depicting Christ with children is in memory of the Alexander family. A window on the east side shows Christ with Mary and Martha, and is in memory of T.D. Elliott and his son Clarence.

In 1968 the members of the church renovated and refurnished the chancel in celebration of the 126th anniversary of the church. The church was again renovated and expanded in 1986.

REVEREND JOSEPH WHEELER

Reverend Joseph Wheeler was born in England. He came to Canada at age 27 and became a skilled blacksmith and carriage-maker. On July 27, 1837, he became minister for Bolton's Congregational Church.

In 1843 the Congregational Church trustees bought part of Mr. Pexham's property on the north side of Queen Street (where the townhouses are going in). A mud-brick church was constructed, with Reverend Wheeler as pastor. Later the mud-brick church was taken down and a frame building was erected in its place. Reverend Wheeler had a hobby of building pipe organs and he installed a splendid one in the new church.

Reverend Wheeler's salary was donated by the church members and friends. It was a bag of flour, a side of pork, or occasionally one shilling. The salary mattered little to Reverend Wheeler, so he gave it to the needy in the district.

The Reverend used to tell a funny story about Jack McDonald, when the boy was 12. During one of his sermons, Reverend Wheeler noticed Jack poking his finger in Billy Robinson's fiery red hair. Jack held the finger there a few seconds, then pounded his hand on the back of the pew as a blacksmith would pound a hot poker.

Reverend Wheeler died in 1878, and soon after his death the church members dispersed. When the church was demolished, the material was used to build William Newlove's house on Nancy Street. The parsonage was located at 88 King Street East and was torn down in 1952.

This is Rev. Joseph Wheeler, who was pastor of the Bolton Congregational Church until he died in 1878.

THE DUFFY HOME

The last solid timber of the still standing Duffy farm home was set firmly in place as the inhabitants, Mrs. Eliza Duffy and her sons James and Robert, from Ireland, looked on. This sturdy building, constructed on 100 acres of Crown deed land on the Albion 6th Line, was purchased for 67 pounds, 10 shillings, and was completely surrounded by wilderness.

The Duffy home also had the distinction of being the first place of Wesleyan Methodist preaching for various congregations in Albion. After three years as the Wesleyan gathering place, a building of large perimeter was erected in 1848 on the corner of King and Nancy streets, and designated the new (Zion) church. The Old Wesleyan congregation met here recurrently for 28 years, until the site of its final relocation was found and a new church was built in 1876.

Meanwhile Mrs. Duffy and her family settled and farmed the land, enduring many trials, such as the loss of a husband and father, the many hours of manual labour, and the general hardships that accompanied the life of the early settler. The life affected Mrs. Duffy most severely, for she suffered from severe rheumatism and was confined to her house for the last seven years of her life.

However, the farm continued to operate, for she had sold the property to her sons. Thus, in the 142 years it has stood, this simple log farmhouse has achieved its own distinct place in Bolton's rural and religious history.

This is the Duffy home, the first place of Methodist preaching. It still stands on the Albion 6th Line, now clad in brick.

Mrs. Duffy.

The United Church manse was built in 1887.

THE UNITED CHURCH MANSE

The United Church manse was built by Mr. George Watson in 1887. Before this manse was built on Nancy Street and sold to the Methodist Church, the Methodist parsonage had been a home on King Street.

The new brick manse had seven rooms, and there were horse stables and a carpenter's shop just out back of the house. Since 1887, many alterations have been made, modernizing this home to comfortably accommodate the many United Church ministers and their families.

Since the church union between Presbyterians, Methodists and Congregationalists in 1925, the official name of the building has been changed from parsonage to manse. This union of denominations was quite controversial at the time, and Bolton's Presbyterians were lucky, seeing as some of the more reluctant-to-join members did not lose their church, which still stands today. The people who did not join the United Church were called Continuing Presbyterians.

CAVEN PRESBYTERIAN CHURCH

The Presbyterian congregation formed around 1838 and conducted their services in homes and barns. Later they began to meet in the schoolhouse S.S. 2 Albion, which at that time was on the Albion 5th Line at the northwest corner of Lot 3, Concession 5.

A building site for the church was obtained in 1856. This site was on the Goodfellow farm on the southwest corner of Sideroad 5 and the 6th Line. The first Presbyterian church, in the form of a small frame building, was completed that same year.

In 1875 the church was moved from this lot, and the new brick structure was erected at its present location on King Street West. This church was named the Caven Presbyterian Church in memory of a Knox College professor in Toronto by the name of Caven.

Caven Presbyterian Church and manse in winter.

This is the library which was located on the corner of King and Queen streets. In 1895 the library was moved again, to the James Stork residence.

BOLTON PUBLIC LIBRARY

As early as the 1830s Bolton had a library to provide assistance to those who were seeking to improve their education and to provide help to those attempting to obtain a basic understanding of the three R's. These programs were run under the direction of the Mechanics Institute Association until 1879, when they ceased due to lack of pupils. Because the Bolton Public School was utilizing only three of its four classrooms, the vacant room became the new library in 1882. It was also run by the Mechanics Institute. The highly capable librarian, a Captain Booth, offered services in the evenings, which the public made good use of. During this time the library paid 12 1/2 cents per night plus additional fees for the use of the space to the school board. Although a fee might seem unusual, it was used to subsidize a row of soft maple trees planted beside the Albert Street school.

Due to Bolton's increasing literary interest, the library was relocated to the rear of the building at King and Queen streets, where it continued to aid the community. An act proclaiming that power should be given to directors of institutes so that they could move reading rooms and book collections to municipal councils was passed in 1895. Thus, the need to transfer the library once again surfaced, and it was moved to the James Stork residence. Nancy Stork claimed the title of librarian from David W. Hughes, who had held that post for a number of years. Also due to the act, the library was officially named the Bolton Public Library.

BOLTON POST OFFICE

George Bolton was the first postmaster in Bolton, from 1832 to 1834. During 1835 Samuel Sterne was postmaster, and during 1836 J. Bolton held the position. In 1837 Samuel Sterne took the job once again and remained postmaster until 1841. There are no records available from 1842-1851.

In 1852 Samuel Walford became postmaster. At this time the post office was located on the north side of King Street West. Walford held the job until 1867, when George Evans took over. He located the post office in his hotel, the Queen's, until he retired in January 1881.

This is the post office building that Byron Leavens erected on Queen Street North. The Daines added the top portion, where they resided during their tenure as postmasters.

In March 1881 Samuel Snell became postmaster and relocated the post office in his drugstore at the corner of King and Queen streets. Later he moved it to Jennie Bell's home beside the Queen's Hotel. Snell retired in February 1908.

In April 1908 Lincoln Hutton took over the job. He built a new post office on Queen Street between Cameron's store and O.J. Hardwick's casino. Hutton retired in March 1927.

Byron Leavens became postmaster in September 1927. At this time the post office was located in Leggett and Smith's drugstore. During his tenure as postmaster he erected a new building on the east side of Queen Street North. Leavens died in January 1945 and his wife became postmistress for two years.

In February 1947 Mr. and Mrs. C.F. Daines took over the position. In 1962 the post office was moved to a new building on King Street West, which is its present location. In 1972 it was enlarged to its present size. The Daines retired from their positions in 1973, and Connie Vanstone was acting postmistress until 1986, when the present postmaster, Fred Warsley, took over the position.

BOLTON TOWN HALL

The present site of the Town Hall was the original location of the Primitive Methodist Church. The hall was used for services until the Methodists united, around 1901. At this time the village purchased the building for use as the Town Hall, replacing the original on Nancy Street. During WWI the Bolton Red Cross organized the town's drive to collect items for packages for the soldiers overseas. Meetings were held in the Town Hall to collect and package the donations. Outside was the farmer's market, held every Monday. Buyers came from Toronto to buy eggs, butter and produce. The market flourished until 1927, when motor cars arrived.

In 1906 a small jail with two cells was established in the hall to house railway workers who celebrated too heartily on payday.

In 1915 a short course of the Junior Farmers was presented here by J.A. Carroll. This was shortly after the Junior Farmers was organized. Once the Ontario Minister of Agriculture, the Hon. Manning Doherty, addressed Bolton residents at the Town Hall.

In January 1918 a theatrical version of Uncle Tom's Cabin was presented at the hall by a group from Toronto, admission 25 cents. In May 1918 a large concert was held at the hall, featuring comedian William J. White, monologist and pianist E. Iles Brazil and baritone H. Ruthvan McDonald. Also that May, the Hepworth League of Macville presented The Minister's Wife's New Bonnet on behalf of the Red Cross, who were desperately in need of funds. Canadian residents over 16 were required to register in 1918, and local registrations took place in the hall. Thomas Childs was caretaker and was paid an annual salary of $35.

On March 12, 1920, the members of the village council voted to insure the hall against fire: $1,350 for the building and $150 for the furniture.

Just one year later, on Monday, May 9, 1921, at 12:45 p.m., fire broke out. Only the brick walls were saved. The town was saved from fire by hoses attached to a cistern at the Imperial Bank and a bucket chain from the Queen's Hotel. On Monday, June 16, a meeting was held to discuss the establishment of a new hall. On January 13, 1922, Robert Caldwell met the council to discuss the new Town Hall's construction. A contract was set up on April 12. The new hall cost $5,000, not including heating and furniture. The new building had a basement at ground level housing council chambers. The walls were raised three feet to allow for an auditorium with increased seating capacity. The reopening of the hall was November 28, 1922. A large concert was organized with local and out-of-town talent.

The hall was the home of the Rebekahs' bazaar and their annual amateurs' night. For several years the town library was located here, and the fire engines were kept inside the doors on Chapel Street beside the police station.

During the late 1920s and early 30s, the Junior Farmers formed a drama group, and one of their productions was attended by Lucy Maud Montgomery, author of the Anne of Green Gables series. Also, the Rotary Club held their meetings here.

During the late 1940s and early 50s, Mr. Ken Cockerill operated a movie house at the hall. In 1951 the auditorium returned to being a community entertainment hall. The three churches of Bolton used the hall for HiTeen meetings. This group presented Buddy in the hall and in neighbouring communities. The Community Choir held shows at the hall in the 1950s.

In the early 1960s, the ambulance was parked inside the large doors on Chapel Street. The council chambers moved in 1967 to the municipal offices on Mill Street, the former location of Plummer's foundry. At this time the hall was sold to a private citizen, and then sold again. Since that time the Town Hall has housed various businesses, such as a sheet metal shop, a bicycle shop, and most recently a fish and chips shop.

This is a recent photo of the Town Hall. The building was erected in 1922.

Reeves of Bolton. Back row, left to right: James Wolfe 1878-79; Bryan Dowling 1882; Thomas Fisher 1883; Alfred Doig 1884-85; H.H. Bolton 1886-88; D.A. Kennedy 1889. Fourth row, left to right: John McEwen 1890-91; Samuel Snell 1892-93; George Coates 1894-95; J.F. Warbrick 1896-97; David Pearcy 1898; James Clarke 1899-1900; William Beamish 1901-02; O.M. Hodson 1903-05; Arthur McFall 1906-08. Third row, left to right: Henry Rutherford 1909, 1912; S.A. Egan 1910-11; Lambert Bolton 1875-77, 1880-81; Hilliard Allan 1965-72; Frank Leavens 1913-15; E.A. Walshaw 1916-19. Second row, left to right: D.B. Kennedy 1920-23; Robert Smith 1924-28, 1951-52; P.W. McMurter 1928-30, 1933-40; Cecil Gott 1941-45; O.J. Hardwick 1946-51; O.H. Downey 1952-53. Bottom row, left to right: James Goodfellow 1954-55; Alex McCauley 1956; Wilton Downey 1957-62; Robert Bulloch 1963-64.

REEVES OF BOLTON

Many of the reeves of Bolton held prominent positions in town businesses. Some served on town council or were deputy-reeves before being promoted to reeve. Bolton had 30 reeves from 1872 until 1972, when it was taken in as the Region of Peel, making reeves no longer necessary.

Bolton's first reeve was Lambert R. Bolton. He was reeve from 1875-77 and 1880-81. Lambert was the eldest grandson of Bolton's founder, James Bolton. Lambert also ran as the Liberal candidate in Cardwell riding but lost to the Hon. J.H. Cameron, a Conservative.

James Wolfe was reeve from 1878-79. He was captain of the No. 4 Company Volunteers. James also gave notice of the bill incorporating the Village of Bolton on June 3, 1872, with a population of 795.

Bryan Dowling was reeve of Bolton in 1882. He was also Bolton's first railway agent.

H.H. Bolton was reeve from 1886-88. H.H. was a lawyer. In 1888 he bought the town newspaper, then known as the British Standard. He changed the name to the Bolton Enterprise. H.H. had no experience in this business, so he hired Frank Leavens (reeve from 1912-15) to manage the plant. Leavens bought the plant from H.H. Bolton in 1893.

D.A. Kennedy and John McEwen were reeves in 1884 and 1890-1891 respectively. Both men were butchers.

Samuel Snell was reeve from 1892-93. He was a druggist and for a time Bolton's postmaster.

George Coates was reeve from 1894-95. He was one of Bolton's blacksmiths.

J.F. Warbrick was reeve from 1896-97. He was greatly interested in the improvement of the village and township. His father, James Warbrick, owned the tannery on the north side of Queen Street (where the townhouses are now located) in 1848.

James Clarke was Bolton's first twentieth-century reeve, from 1899-1900. He bought John Gardhouse's store in 1881.

William Beamish was reeve from 1901-02. His father, John Beamish, was a drover and a butcher. In 1890 William and his brother Ernest took over the business. William was also manager of T. Eaton Company's meat department in Toronto for a time.

Arthur McFall was reeve from 1906-08. His father, Andrew McFall, bought the mill from John Gardhouse in 1881. Arthur took over in 1894. Arthur was very interested in the welfare and improvement of the village. He installed and operated an electric light plant, until the advent of the hydro system. Arthur was a strong promoter of the Bolton Telephone Company.

E.A. Walshaw was reeve from 1916-19. His father, Joshua Walshaw, was owner of Walshaw's Woollen Mills. When Joshua retired in 1902, Edward took over the business and continued until 1923, when the mill burned down.

Reeve Otto J. Hardwick

P.W. McMurter was reeve from 1928-30 and from 1933-40. He was the owner of the first barber shop in Bolton, in 1908.

O.J. Hardwick was one of the most popular men in town and was reeve from 1946-51. O.J. was coach of Bolton's hockey team and manager of the Hickman Street arena. He was also president of the Jamboree Committee. O.J. established the dairy in 1934 and started the first pasturizing plant in this district. He built the Bolton Cold Storage Lockers once located at the corner of Queen and Mill streets. O.J. also operated the Bolton Casino, which was beside Bolton Florists. He was killed in a car accident while coming home from a hockey game. Hardwick Road is named for him.

O.H. Downey and Wilton Downey were reeves from 1952-53 and 1957-62 respectively. Their ancestor William Downey holds the distinction of being the first white man to sleep overnight in Albion Township, in 1819. Downey Drive on the South Hill is named for them.

James Goodfellow was reeve from 1954-55. He was owner of the mill for a time.

Alex McCauley was reeve in 1956. During his time as reeve, street signs were purchased and erected with the assistance of the Chamber of Commerce.

Robert Bulloch was reeve from 1963-64. He was the owner of Bulloch's IGA.

Hilliard Allan was Bolton's last reeve, from 1965-72. He holds the honour of being reeve for the longest term. He was the owner of the Bolton Dairy from 1948-73. Allan Drive on the South Hill is named for him.

This is the inside of P.W. McMurter's barber shop, which was located where the Towne Shoppe is today. McMurter's shop was opened to serve Bolton in 1908. Mr. McMurter was reeve of Bolton on two occasions, from 1928 to 1930, and from 1933-1940. In this picture, Mr. McMurter can be seen at left. Prior to 1908, Harry Sheardown was barber for many years.

The Temperance Hall schoolhouse can be seen in this picture. The school is the building to the right. It is situated at the southeast corner of John and Victoria streets. The building to the left still stands on John Street.

THE TEMPERANCE HALL SCHOOL

On March 24, 1858, the Temperance Hall (which was located on the southeast corner of John and Victoria streets) was purchased by the Sons of Temperance from John Helliwell for $75. Just over two years later, in September 1860, the Temperance Hall was sold to the Bolton School Board to use as a schoolhouse.

The first headmaster, at age 23, was Thomas Elliott. He was hired in 1865. His assistant was Miss Mary Foster, and collectively the two taught the 245 scholars enrolled.

Two new teachers were hired in September 1867 to replace the former two. A learned Scotsman, Peter McTavish, became headmaster, and his daughter, Miss Margaret McTavish, taught in a second room which had been set up to try to lessen crowding of the 250 pupils.

Here are the estimated operating expenses for the Temperance Hall school:

Balance on mortgage and interest	$206
Balance on property	40
Teachers' salaries	280
Cleaning school	16
Wood	14
Cutting and splitting wood	4
School tax collector	5
Fixing stoves	10
Total	$575

In 1869 Thomas Elliot returned to the school as headmaster with his new assistant, Eliza Bolton, the niece of Mr. James Bolton, for whom the town is named.

The year 1873 brought many meetings of the Bolton School Board (about three per month) to discuss the increasing student population. Their solution was to make a few minor repairs and alterations to create a third room. Of course a new teacher was needed for this third room, so Miss R.A. Clarke was hired. The new classroom was finished in May 1873. "Finished" included buying a third water pail and some cups for the school.

The final decision was that a larger school was necessary. When the Albert Street school was built, in 1874, the Temperance Hall school was no longer used, after 14 years of service.

On February 27, 1875, during a public auction, the lot and building were sold to George Elliott for $249. The sale did not include the school bell, which greatly disappointed Mr. Elliott. The old bell was used in the new school on Albert Street. The Temperance Hall, which was sold to James Goodfellow, became a barn. Finally, the structure was dismantled and the sturdy beams were brought to Mr. Goodfellow's property by the mill, where he used them in construction of a seed plant, which was located close to the east bank of the Humber River, at the bridge.

Here is the Albert Street school as it was in earlier days, with its classes standing out front.

JAMES BOLTON PUBLIC SCHOOL

It was December 27, 1968, and the snow was still falling heavily as flames slowly crept up the east-end stairwell of the Albert Street school. Before the night was through, the building had been engulfed by flames, causing $25,000 in damage and leaving behind only smouldering remnants of what had started out as a four-room schoolhouse in 1874.

Back then, the building had stood proudly amidst the lush greenery, offering an education from grades 1 to 8, and, to comply with regulations of the time, a separation of males and females in school and on the playgrounds. As the years progressed, the school underwent numerous changes: in 1920 hydro was installed; in 1921 pipeless furnaces were built in each classroom, surely a welcome relief, especially during the cold winter months; in 1923, in order to accommodate the needs of a growing community, two classrooms and a basement were added. This allowed grades 1-8 to be taught in the lower level while grades 9-12 were taught upstairs.

As the number of students attending the Albert Street school steadily increased to 200, additional staff was required, and several new teachers were hired so that the students could get the education they needed. Even so, numerous pupils were absent on a regular basis in the spring and fall, for Bolton was still basically a farming community.

Bolton School Board. Left to right: Chairman Donald Kennedy, Secretary John McDonald, David Wilson, William Stubbs, Alsey Norton, Ernie Beamish, (William Beamish not present).

Because the Albert Street school was becoming quite prominent, Murray Hesp suggested they change the name to the James Bolton School, in honour of the founder of the village, and this was promptly accomplished.

In 1957 the school once again felt the need to expand its facilities, thus another wing containing additional classrooms, bathrooms and a teachers' lounge, was added.

From the first day of school in 1874, as Principal P. Elliott watched the excited children clamber into the $5,000 building, to the last, as Principal E. McDonald reminisced as flames seared up the building, the James Bolton School played a major role in educating the community of Bolton.

1930 Room 1 classes. Left to right, top row: Thornton Bell, Bob Studholme, Henry McCabe, John Hesp, Garfield Lippin, Pearl McLennan, Frances Bellchamber, Frances Hesp, Clara Lippin, Irene Carey, Phyllis Ellwood, Helen Maxwell, Miss Lorna Guy. Second row from top: Eileen Jones, Freda Kirby, Barbara McCauley, Eria Studholme, Mina Godfrey, Ronald Greenwood, John Sheardown, Roger Pilson. Third row from top: Louie Pilson, Allan McCort, Glenda Stephenson, Ethel Stubbs, Erma Watts, Eileen Smith, Betty Barry, *(the four children on the right have not yet been identified)*. Bottom row: Earl Stewart, Tom Laurie, Rooney Cleaver, Cecil Floyd, Sandy Laurie, Mackey Keetch, Lorne Sheardown, Billy Keetch, Jim Maw.

On December 27, 1968, James Bolton P.S. burned down.

Flood photo showing the bottom of the Humberlea, 1912.

FLOODS

Those who have resided in Bolton for a long period of time are well aware that there were floods in the spring and sometimes fall of practically every year. Some of the more significant floods occurred in 1865, 1911, 1912, and during Hurricane Hazel in 1954.

The flood of 1865 came as no surprise following a cold, harsh winter of extremely heavy snowfall. Due to the sudden onset of spring in the first week in April, the ice below the dam began to melt. Soon it became dislodged and started to travel downstream as far as Charles Bolton's house, where it became stuck due to the narrowness of the river at this point. Forming an enormous ice jam, it forced the Humber River to back up, thus flooding a large part of the village. In addition to this, the unusually thick ice above the Queen Street Bridge split into large segments and, being unable to pass through the piles, forced the river down Queen Street. One can clearly see why the 1865 flood was by far one of the worst Bolton has ever experienced.

The flood of 1911 also came following a harsh winter, though its exact cause is unknown. Although not as many miles were flooded, the east end of Bolton was entirely under water—"from the mill down to the hill was all under water."

The flood of 1912 occurred on April 7. It came following a Siberian winter and raised the water level of the Humber River to unaccustomed heights. Once again, huge blocks of ice were split as though they were made of sand. As can be seen

Firth Jaffary and Ollie Downey canoeing down Mill Street (1942).

in the picture, these ice floes were pushed onto the shore, creating jams and much damage. Surprisingly, these ice floes created a new type of sport. A cake would be pried off the shore or the mill bridge, and a couple of people would set it in the river, then jump on. Carried by the river current, they would continue downstream until they reached the low-lying bridge. Here they would run across the bridge and attempt to jump back on the floe. If unsuccessful they would go down in four metres of icy water.

Hurricane Hazel was definitely one of the most severe storms ever to hit Bolton. It struck in the fall of 1954, its only forewarning being the uneasiness of the animals in the village. Accompanied by furious winds and with rain literally pouring from the sky, it left behind a trail of wreckage, a flooded village, and memories that would last a lifetime.

This photo shows William Bell standing across from the Mill Street foundry during the 1942 flood. His house is at the centre of the picture.

As Willow Street floods, so does the home of Mrs. Francis Robinson, grandmother of Elizabeth Downey (1942).

This picture of Robertson Matthews was taken in his home at 45 Willow Street. (The house is still standing.) Mr. Matthews was not only the subject of the photograph, but also the photographer, with the help of time lapse photography. He was quite involved in photography and was no doubt one of the first to take pictures around Bolton. Starting around 1900 he took photos using glass plates. In his day, Robertson Matthews could often be seen taking long walks around the village. He was well known and one of the most highly regarded photographers of the time.

MR. ROBERTSON MATTHEWS

Robertson Matthews was born in Toronto in 1880 to Reverend Matthew H. Matthews and his wife, Naomi. His father was a circuit preacher who served the Bolton area.

Robertson Matthews attended Allegheny College in Pennsylvania and Cornell University in Ithaca, New York. At Cornell he received his doctorate in Mechanical Engineering and eventually accepted a teaching position. In 1913 he married Ethel Matthews (nee Dodds).

During WWI he was a leading authority on internal combustion engines in the United States. While he was in the States, he chose to become an American citizen. However he returned to Bolton in 1931 to care for his ailing mother, and to recover after a serious auto accident. Mr. Matthews remained in Canada until his death in 1972 at Peel Manor in Brampton.

This is a photo of Naomi Matthews, mother of Robertson Matthews. She is seen here with her walking wheel--aptly named, for the operators had to stand while working with it.

This picture most likely was taken by Robertson Matthews. The date of the photo is circa 1916. The fisherwomen are Matthews' wife and sister.

Another photo probably taken by Matthews. It was taken behind the McFall home (now the Goodfellow residence) on King Street East. Mr. Matthews is the gentleman playing croquet. His wife, Edith, is standing to the extreme right. What do you think the ladies are planning?

Orange Day Parade, July 12, 1911. Note Jaffary's in the background.

THE ORANGE DAY PARADE

The robust sound of the Cadet Band playing some fine selections could be heard every year on July 12 as they headed the parade marching down King Street. The Orange Day Parade, enjoyed greatly by the citizens of Bolton, was appropriately named for the Bolton Orange Lodge. Founded in 1857 when a warrant was issued to Hugh Abercrombie, the club originally had 58 members and made a real community effort by starting the parade on July 12 of that same year. The parade was a tremendous success and became a regular part of the July 12 festivities in the 1860s. As one can see from the crowds that turned out (photo), people of various ages attended, all displaying the "haute couture" of the times. This meant long, white dresses and flowery hats (and a parasol if necessary) for the women, and trousers, white shirts, and Homburg hats for the men. All in all, the Orange Day Parade was a well-liked form of entertainment enjoyed by many.

BOLTON BAND

The band was a vital part of all communities. Bolton's band is believed to have been formed in 1885. The first bandleader was David W. Hughes. He carried on as leader until 1893, when John Wood arrived from Lloydtown to become leader. Wood's daughter, Maude, played cornet in this band, which was considered a novelty at the time. The next leader was Tommy Miller, who worked at Walshaw's Woollen Mills. After Miller left the band, he became the leader of Brandon, Manitoba's band.

For a while there were two bands in Bolton, the brass band and another one led by James McDonald.

In 1904 a banker named Maguire organized a band that lasted two years. In 1907 John T. Galvin organized an impressive band with uniforms. They had annual outings to Owen Sound, Parry Sound, Bala, Peterborough, St. Thomas and elsewhere. This band carried on until 1914, when James McDonald formed the next band. It did such things as lead the parades when the boys returned home from WWI. Around 1933 McDonald gathered more recruits for another band that he called the Beginners' Band. It really was meant for beginners, but McDonald couldn't prevent the older men from joining too. The next leader was William J. Heffernan from Lindsay, Ontario. He was leader from 1938-1941. Heffernan was responsible for starting the Bolton Jamboree. His band travelled to such places as Newmarket, Georgetown, Acton, Brampton and Alliston. From 1942 to 1944 James Napier from Toronto was bandmaster. During his time there were ladies as members. They were Ruth Stubbs, Bernice Maw, Isobel Stewart, Nellie Pilson, Edith Beauchamp and Christine Pegg.

The band was discontinued in 1945.

Bolton Band. Front row, left to right: John Beamish, B-flat alto; D.W. Hughes, B-flat cornet; George Brown, E-flat alto; Job Hughes, B-flat bass; Fred Bolton, E-flat bass; Harvey Elliot, snare drum. Back row, left to right: Henry Bolton, baritone; Charles Plummer, E-flat cornet; Robert Russell, piccolo; John Noble, B-flat cornet; Sidney Northcott, E-flat alto.

The Bolton Citizen's Band.

Shown is the Bolton Fair Grounds, reproduced from a postcard. The Fair is an important part of Bolton social life.

THE BOLTON FAIR

The Bolton Fall Fair was and still is a focal point in entertainment for Bolton. Founded by the thriving Bolton Agricultural Society in 1860, it quickly became well known for features such as dancing grizzly bears and various circus acts. Renovated circa 1865-70, the grounds were expanded to include a one-third-mile race track, to which some of the most magnificent horses in the country were brought to test their speed. The early presidents of the Fair were:

Charles Barrett	1857-1866
William Rogers	1867
Joseph Newlove	1868
George Verner	1869
James Wolfe	1870
William Dick	1871-1872
Alex McCabe	1873-1877
Isaac Wilson	1878-1879
Albert Dodds	1880
W.S. Buist	1881-1882
Thomas Calley	1883-1889
Thomas Swinarton	1890-1891

Thanks to people like these and the community of Bolton, the Fair has been a flourishing attraction for over 125 years and will continue to be one in the future.

THE ROYAL CANADIAN LEGION, BOLTON BRANCH

The Legion was formed by veterans of WWI and WWII. In 1945 a meeting was held at the Town Hall to explain what the Legion was all about. They also picked the executive board. The Bolton branch of the Royal Canadian Legion received charter #371 in June 1946. The members at that time were Harry Carter (President), Ted Edwards, John Whitbread, Ernest Robertson, L.K. Cockerill, Grant Cameron, E.A. George, Arnold Thompson, Dr. D.A. Wylie, Roy Hesp, A. Ennis, W.A. Gordon, E.J. Wilson, C. Pegg, and J.J. Robbins.

The attic above Schaefer's hardware (now Cowieson's) on Queen Street was used for their meetings. In 1950-51 they held fund-raisers such as a car raffle and a food locker raffle to raise money to purchase a house on Ann Street (across from the present Legion). From 1951-61 the Legion members sold bonds. They purchased land and began the first stage of the present Legion in June 1961. An addition was added in July 1972.

THE LADIES AUXILIARY

The Ladies Auxiliary received their charter on November 22, 1960. The members at the time were Mae Lockhart, Alice Roden, Sarah Whitbread, Alma Surette, Mary Pilson, Bonnie

Schaeffer, Norma Groat, Isabel Matheson, Mildred Lockhart, Gertrude McDowell, Mildred Whitehead, Grace Robb, Iola Palmer, Viola Corless, Minnie Hesp, Helen Traynor, Jean Schild, Beatrice Bateman, Margaret Richardson, Anne Walton, Mary Jackson, Muriel Dinwoodie, and Pearl Morrison.

THE BOLTON CAMP

One is constantly reading about the high level of pollution in cities, and how often city people don't have anywhere to go to get some fresh air. One tends to take things such as rolling hills, leafy green trees, and clean, fresh air for granted if one lives in the country. As hard as it is to believe, the factors mentioned were already taking their toll in the early 1900s. Seeking to solve this growing problem, a group of men from Toronto decided to build a summer camp for city children, and so bought a relatively small piece of land on the outskirts of Bolton in 1929. Tents were added to the house and building, called a clubhouse, already on site, and the area was considered ready for the first group of campers. Mr. R. Pilson was the first caretaker, and after him came Mr. H. Byrnes. Under the supervision of Mr. Byrnes, cabins were built to take the place of the tents, the grounds were cleaned, and trees and flowers were planted. The sight of such an inviting camp must have cheered up the campers, almost all of whom had to walk all the way from the railway station.

During the course of Mr. Byrnes' 27-year leadership, the Bolton Camp was divided into four different sections, so that many different city-dwellers could attend, not just children. The Sherbourine section was for girls, the Rotary for boys, the Hastings section for mothers and babies, and the Howell section for mothers and children. Each of these sections was like a camp contained within a larger one, for they all contained their own kitchen, dining room, swimming pool, recreation room, craft house, medical unit, and playground.

From the first excited children wondering at the tents to the last group of mothers and children playing together in the recreation room, to have been a camper at Bolton Camp was an honour for all, and the experiences shared there were remembered for a lifetime.

The Bolton Fresh Air Camp was a popular place for children to "get away to the country."

Roller boat.

THE SUNDAY MORNING CLASS

Champions.

The sound of hard leather balls cracking against strong wooden bats was not unfamiliar to the members of the Senior Girls Softball Team, better known as the "Sunday Morning Class." Founded through the hard work of Principal A.C. Fowler of Bolton Public School in May 1924, this baseball team would go on to win one championship after another. The original team, consisting of Hilda Doupe, Helen Crossett, Clara McCallum, Evelyn Wallace, Margaret Armstrong, Gertrude Hurron, Olive Henderson, Gladys Henderson, Mabel Beamish, May Fuller, and the team mascot, Olive McCallum, would go on to an undefeated season in 1924.

Every Saturday they played teams from Toronto, some of the games taking place at the prestigious Toronto Exhibition Park. The team always managed to look its best, not only through their playing, but also due to their uniforms. How could they not, with navy blue bloomers, white sweaters and striped navy ties?

In September 1925 the "Sunday Morning Class" won the Toronto and District Championship by putting the Oshawa Pirates to shame with a 19-8 score. So continued the successes of this renowned baseball team until the club was dismantled in 1928, after it had added titles such as Champions of the Inter-Peel-Simcoe Girls' Indoor Baseball League and Winners of the York-Peel-Simcoe Tournament to its credit. The many hours of practice and coaching worked well to create a champion baseball team from the group of young women who called themselves the "Sunday Morning Class."

Hockey Team. Top left, Harry Sheardown. Fifth from left, George Norton. Bottom left, Stewart Cameron. Bottom right, Elwyn Elliott.

DID YOU KNOW...

...that for years Shore Street was known as Short Street? In Bolton's centennial year, 1972, the spelling was found to be an error on the original map.

...that Albert Street was named for Prince Albert, Royal Consort of Queen Victoria?

...that Allan Drive was named for Hilliard Allan, who ran the Bolton Dairy from 1948-1973 and was Bolton's last reeve?

...that Ann Street was named for Ann Sterne, whose husband operated a distillery, and that they both contributed land for the first Anglican church?

...that Centennial Drive was formerly part of Highway 50 but was changed in 1963 and renamed at Bolton's Centennial, 1972?

...that Chapel Street was named for the Primitive Methodist chapel located here until it was replaced in 1873 by the Town Hall?

...that Connaught Crescent was named for the Duke of Connaught, Queen Victoria's son and Canada's Governor-General from 1911-1916?

...that Crestwood Road was so named simply because it is situated on the crest of a hill near a wooded ravine?

...that Dalton Street was named for Dr. William Henry Dalton, a highly respected doctor who practised in Bolton from 1860-1875?

...that David Street was named for David Norton, who operated a brickmaking business at the south end of the street? The narrow street was the lane where they used to bring out the bricks.

...that Dingle Court was named for C. Robert Dingle, a school board trustee and a town council member?

...that Downey Drive was named for Wilton and Orland Downey, whose Bolton ancestors date back to 1819, when William Downey was the first white man to sleep overnight in Albion Township? And did you know that it was originally called Walker Court?

...that Ellwood Drive was named for William and James Ellwood, who were killed in WWII?

...that Forest Court was so named because it is beside a hillside forest?

...that Foundry Court was so named because Dick's Foundries were located here?

...that George Street was named for King George V, King of Great Britain and Ireland?

...that Glasgow Road extends through a suburb of Bolton that was once called Glasgow?

...that Glenwood Crescent was so named because it overlooks a wooded glen?

...that Grace Court was named for Grace Maida, wife of Domenic Maida, who was the developer of this area?

...that Haines Drive was named for Alberta Haines, granddaughter of David Norton, the owner of the brickyard?

...that Hardwick Road was named for Otto J. Hardwick, an impressive leader of athletics in Bolton and owner of several businesses?

...that Healey Road was named for Fergus Healey, an astute businessman in town?

...that Henderson Street was named for the Henderson family who once farmed the area?

...that Hersey Crescent was named for E.D. Hersey, Clerk-Treasurer for Bolton from 1962-73?

...that Hesp Drive was named for three generations of Hesps who farmed the area?

...that Hickman Street was named for Dr. Hickman, a prominent doctor whose house was situated on this street in 1872?

...that Hilltop Court was so named simply because it is on the top of a hill?

...that Humber Lea Road was so named because it extends south toward the Humber River valley?

...that James Street was named for James C. Bolton, founder of Bolton? He started the first mill, the first store and built the first frame house.

...that King Street was named for the King of England?

...that Kingsview Drive was once called Godbolt Drive, but that the name was changed because there were objections?

...that Leavens Court was named as a compliment to the Leavens family, who have been associated with the *Enterprise* since November 15, 1888?

...that Leonard Street, Martha Street and Crescent, and Pearl Street were all named for members of the Henderson family who farmed this area?

...that Little Crescent was so named simply because it is a little court?

...that Louisa Street was named for Louisa Bolton, daughter of Lambert Bolton, the first reeve? And did you know that it was sometimes called "Green Lane" because of the overhanging tree branches?

... that Lydia Street was named for Lydia Haynes-Jenkins, whose husband owned and developed land in this area?

... that Maidstone Court was named for Domenic Maida, the area's developer?

... that Marple Crescent was named for Ralph Marple, who was a member of the Bolton Council from 1968-73?

... that Meadowvale Court was so named simply because it is located in a meadow?

... that Mellow Crescent was named for the Mellow family, early settlers in the north of Bolton?

... that Mill Street was so named because Bolton Mill was located on the road's bend?

... that Murray Lane was named for Murray Hawkins, a Bolton councillor from 1957-1959?

... that Nancy, Jane and Elizabeth streets were all named for daughters of James C. Stork, an early Bolton councillor?

... that Newlove Drive was named for William J. Newlove, a former Bolton councillor and deputy-reeve?

... that Norton Boulevard was named for the Norton family who operated the brickyard and farmed in this area?

... that Piercey Road was named for Newton and Carmen Piercey, local farmers?

... that Queen and Victoria streets were named in honour of Queen Victoria?

... that Ridge Road, Ridgebank and Ridgewood Courts were so named because they were situated on a ridge?

... that Sackville Street was named for Thomas Sackville, first Earl of Dorset?

... that Sherin Court was named for Sherin Maida, daughter of the developer of this area, Domenic Maida?

... that Shore Street was named in honour of the Shore family, who were early settlers in Bolton?

... that Station Road was so named because of its proximity to the C.P.R. station?

... that Stephen Drive was named for Stephen Hartwick, who father, C.W., built the Hilltop Shopping Plaza and the houses on the west side of Queen Street?

... that Temperance Street was named for the Temperance Hall once located on the corner of King and Temperance?

. . . that Valleyview Court was so named for its view of the valley?

. . . that William Street was named for King William?

. . . that Wilton Drive was named for Wilton Downey?

. . . that Whitehead Crescent was named for Donald Whitehead, Sr., who operated a General Motors dealership, and for Richard Whitehead, who served as deputy reeve from 1972-1973?

. . . that Woodrow Avenue was named for Gordon Woodrow, last building inspector in Bolton?

. . . that Wright Crescent was named for George Wright, a former member of the Bolton Council and former principal of James Bolton Public School?

. . . that the west arm of Connaught Crescent was once called York Avenue, named for the Duke of York?

. . . that Blanche, Hill, Lockville, Slancy, Susan, Union, and Water streets were all planned but never opened?

. . . that Dick Street, Eliza Street, Lambert Road, Maria Street, Ormistone Street, and Timothy Lane were once roads in Bolton but are now closed?

Mock holdup of Bolton Town Hall by World War II cadets from camp.

Paul Follett, Isabelle Schmelzer, Alanna May, Susanne Baillie, Don Reid.

ACKNOWLEDGEMENTS

Authors
Susanne Baillie
Alanna May
Isabelle Schmelzer

Classmates 1985
Michael Anderson
Hillary Barron
Dianne Burton
Arran Caza
Todd Charbonneau
Matt Chevalier
Jayson Chung
Beth Corkill
Melissa Dingle

Candice Fischer
Valere Grams
Larry Hamson
Jason Jaeger
Helen King
Kristen Nelles
David Soyka
Brent Todd
Lynn Wiegard

Principals
Mr. W. Owens
Mr. D. Weldon

Mr. P. Jones

Teachers 1986
Ms. Pat Adele
Mr. Bill Bogers
Mrs. Karen Van Bemmel

Mrs. Wendy Chalmers
Ms. Jane Kirkpatrick

Project Advisors
Mr. Paul Follett
Mr. Don Reid

Interviewees
Mr. & Mrs. Edgar Bowes
Mrs. Eva Brown
Mr. & Mrs. C. Daines
Mrs. Dingle
Mrs. Susan Doughty
Mr. Harold Egan
Mrs. Eulaila Elliott

Mrs. Edith Ellwood
Mrs. Olive Henderson
Mrs. W. Leavens
Mrs. Doris Porter
Mrs. Sheila Simpson
Mr. & Mrs. Bill Venning
Ms. Dorothy Wakely

Also
Mr. Bill Whitbread and the Bolton *Enterprise*; Mrs. Heather Broadbent; Ms. Beth Early; Mr. G. Crawford; our parents; Region of Peel Archives; the Albion-Bolton Historical Society; the Caledon Heritage Resource Office; Belmont Studios, Bolton; Christ Church, Bolton; the Community of Bolton; and, John Denison and The Boston Mills Press, Erin.

Sorry if we left you out!

INDEX

Abercrombie, Hugh 77
Alexander family 51
Allan, Hilliard 62, 86
Armstrong, Margaret 84

Barry, Alex 19
Bateman, Beatrice 82
Beamish, Ernest 61, 67
Beamish, John 61
Beamish, Mabel 84
Beamish, Richard 11, 17
Beamish, Wm. 61
Beauchamp, Edith 77
Bell, J. 33
Bell, Jennie 33, 49, 58
Bell, Wm. 72
Bolton, Charles 71
Bolton, Ellen 50
Bolton, Eliza 65
Bolton, George 9, 13, 57
Bolton, H.H. 30, 31, 61
Bolton, J.N. 30
Bolton, James C. 9, 13, 50, 57, 61, 65, 87
Bolton, Lambert 9, 33, 39, 61, 87
Bolton, Louisa 87
Booth, Captain 57
Brazil, E. Iles 58
Broetski, Mike 15
Buist, Alexander 27
Buist, William 27
Bulloch, Robert 62
Burton, Edith 35
Byrnes, H. 82

Caldwell, Robert 59
Cameron, Bruce 20
Cameron, Grant 81
Cameron, Hon. J.H. 61
Cameron, Stewart 85
Carroll, J.A. 58
Carter, Harry 81
Case, Charles C. 28
Case, J.I. 32
Caven, Prof. 54
Childs, Thomas 58
Clarke, Frank 15
Clarke, James 11, 20, 61
Clarke, Norman 15
Clarke, Mrs. R.A. 65
Coates, George 61
Cockerill, Ken 59, 81
Collins, Miss Edith 20
Corless, Viola 82
Cowieson, Mr. 28
Crossett, Helen 84
Cusliss, Thomas 11
Curliss, William 11

Daines, Mr. & Mrs. C.F. 57, 58
Dalton, Dr. William Henry 86
Dick, Albert 32
Dick, Alex 32
Dick, Andrew 35
Dick, Florence 35
Dick, T.A. 34, 35
Dick, William 11, 22, 23
Dickson, W.J. 17
Dingle, C. Robert 86
Dinwoody, Muriel 82
Dodds, A. 11, 23, 25
Doherty, Hon. Manning 58

Downey, Clarence 62, 86, 89
Downey, Elizabeth 73
Downey, O.H. 62, 71, 86
Downey, William 62, 86
Downey, Wilton 62, 86, 89
Doupe, Hilda 84
Duffy, Mrs. Eliza 53
Duffy, James 53
Duffy Robert 53
Duncan, Mrs. Bertha 20

Edwards, Ted 81
Egan 17, 23
Elliott, Rev. Adam 50
Elliott, Elwyn 85
Elliott, Helen 15
Elliott, P. 67
Elliott, Robert 31
Elliott, T.D. 15, 51, 65
Ellwood, Mr. 20
Ellwood, James 86
Ellwood, William 86
Ennis, A. 81
Evans, George 11, 15, 16, 57, 65

Fawcett, Mr. 28
Fines, Dan 19
Fisher, Thomas 11
Foster, Miss Mary 65
Fowler, A.C. 84
Fox, Robert 27
Fuller, May 84
Furnace, Howard 23

Galvin, John T. 77
Gardhouse, Mrs. 20
Gardhouse, Fred 20

Gardhouse, John 13, 20, 61
George, E.A. 81
Gooderham, Mr. 31
Goodfellow, James 38, 62, 65
Gordon, W.A. 81
Greshuk, William 15
Grey, Matthew 15
Groat, Norma 81

Haines, Alberta 87
Harper, A.E. 11, 31
Hardwick, Otto J. 58, 62, 87
Harper, Dave 15
Hartwick, C.W. 88
Hartwick, Stephen 88
Hawkins, Murray 88
Hayhoe 13
Haynes-Jenkins, Lydia 88
Healey, Fergus 87
Heffernan, Wm. J. 77
Helliwell, John 65
Henderson, Floyd 15, 87
Henderson, Gladys 84
Henderson, Leonard 87
Henderson, Martha 87
Henderson, Olive 84
Henderson, Pearl 87
Hersey, E.D. 87
Hesp, Minnie 82
Hesp, Murray 67
Hesp, Roy 81, 87
Hickman, Dr. 47, 87
Hickman, Mrs. 47
Hodson, O.M. 5, 28
Honey, Mr. 20
Houston, H.O. (Teddy) 19, 33
Hughes, Mr. 19

Hughes, David W. 57, 77
Hurron, Gertrude 84
Hutchinson, Alex 28
Hutton, Lincoln 58

Jackson, Mary 82
Jaffary, E.A. 11, 18
Jaffary, Edwin 19
Jaffary, Firth 71
Jaffary, Wyatt 19
Jaffary, Wyatt Jr. 19
Johnston, Isabella 51
Johnston, Robert William 51

Kennedy, D.A. 61, 67
Kenyon, R. 11
Kuniski, Mr. 15

Lawson, Edward 13
Leavens, Byron 57, 58
Leavens, F.N. 11, 30, 31, 61
Leavens, Werden 31
Leggett, C.A. 19
Linfoot, T. 17
Lockhart, Mae 81
Lockhart, Mildred 81
Love, Mr. 20
Love, Mrs. 20

Maida, Grace 87
Maida, Dominic 87, 88
Maida, Sherin 88
Maguire, Mr. 77
Marple, Ralph 88
Martin, C.A. 11
Matheson, Isabel 82
Matthews, Ethel 75

Matthews, Rev. Matthew H. 75
Matthews, Naomi 75
Matthews, Robert 74, 75
Maw, Bernice 77
Mellow family 88
Miller, Tommy 77
Morrison, James 15
Morrison, Pearl 82

McCabe, A.E. 10
McCabe, Dr. W.J. 33
McCallum, Clara 84
McCallum, Olive 84
McCauley, Alex 62
McCutcheon, Bill 31
McDonald, E. 67
McDonald, Jack 52
McDonald, James 77
McDonald, John 67
McDowell, Gertrude 81
McEwen, John 61
McFall, Andrew 11, 12, 13
McFall, Arthur 11, 13, 61
McIlroy, Mr. 19
McIntosh, John F. 27
McKee, Mr. 17
McMurter, P.W. 62, 63
McTavish, Miss Margaret 65
McTavish, Peter 65

Napier, James 77
Newlove, William J. 52, 88
Norton, Alsey 14, 15, 67
Norton, David 15, 86, 87
Norton, George 14, 85
Nunn, G. 11

O'Dea, Miss Maggie 20, 21
Osler, Rev. Featherstone Lake 13, 50
Osler, Rev. Henry Bath 47, 50

Pacey, Reg 28
Palmer, Iola 82
Pegg, C. 81
Pegg, Christine 77
Pexham, Mr. 52
Piercey, Carmen 88
Piercey, Newton 88
Pilson, Mary 81
Pilson, Nellie 77
Pilson, R. 82
Plummer, Charles 23, 37
Plummer, J.P. 11, 23
Plummer, William 23
Purvis, Mr. 20

Richardson, Margaret 82
Robb, Grace 81
Robbins, J.J. 81
Robertson, Ernest 81
Robertson, William "Skinny Bill" 14
Robinson, Mr. 28
Robinson, Billy 52
Robinson, Mrs. Francis 73
Roden, Alice 81
Rowley, Kenneth 31
Rowley, Normand 31
Russell, R.I. 33
Russell, R.J. 11

Schaefer, Alex 28, 29
Schaeffer, Bonnie 82

Sheardown, Harry 22, 63, 85
Shild, Jean 82
Small, Daniel 17
Small, Earl 19
Smith, Robert 28, 29
Snell, Samuel J. 19, 58, 61
Squires, J. 17
Staples, Mr. 20
Sterne, Anne 50, 86
Sterne, Boyce 50
Sterne, Samuel 50, 57
Stewart, Andrew 41
Stewart, Dill 41
Stewart, Elizy 41
Stewart, Ernie 41
Stewart, George 41
Stewart, Isobel 77
Stewart, Jim 41
Stewart, Rebecca 41
Stewart, William 14
Stork, James C. 19, 50, 56, 57, 88
Stork, Elizabeth 88
Stork, Jane 88
Stork, Nancy 88
Stubbs, Fred 14
Stubbs, Jimmy 22
Stubbs, Ruth 77
Stubbs, William 67
Surette, Alma 81

Thompson, Arnold 81
Tingley, Mr. 27
Traynor, Helen 82

VanDusen, Mr. 28
Vanstone, Connie 58
Verner, John 36

Walford, Samuel 57
Walshaw, E.A. 61
Walshaw, Edward 27, 61
Walshaw, Joshua 9, 27
Wallace, Evelyn 84
Walton, Anne 82
Warbrick, Daisy 28
Warbrick, John F. 28, 61
Warsley, Fred 58
Watson, George 23, 54
Wheeler, Rev. Joseph 52
Whitbread, John 81
Whitbread, Sarah 81
White, Jack 14
White, William J. 58
Whitehead, Donald Sr. 89
Whitehead, Mildred 82
Whitehead, Richard 89
Williamson, Bob 32
Wilson, David 67
Wilson, E.J. 81
Wilson, Joe 11
Wolfe, James 61
Wood, John 77
Wood, Maude 77
Woodrow, Gordon 89
Wright, George 89
Wylie, Dr. D.A. 81

Pearcy Block was a row of joined buildings at the corner of Queen and Sterne streets. They were owned by David Pearcy, who was reeve in 1898. He had a saddle and harness shop in the block. The furthest left shop was where J.F. Warbrick had Bolton's first bank.

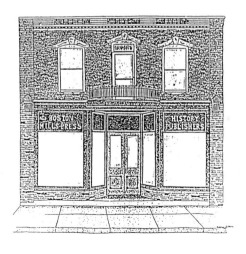

THE BOSTON MILLS PRESS
132 MAIN STREET, ERIN, ONTARIO
1•519•833•2407   FAX 1•519•833•2195